Volcanoes!

TIME
FOR KIDS

D1495265

Cy Armour

Consultant

Timothy Rasinski, Ph.D.
Kent State University

Publishing Credits

Dona Herweck Rice, *Editor-in-Chief*
Robin Erickson, *Production Director*
Lee Aucoin, *Creative Director*
Conni Medina, M.A.Ed., *Editorial Director*
Jamey Acosta, *Editor*
Stephanie Reid, *Photo Editor*
Rachelle Cracchiolo, M.S.Ed., *Publisher*

Based on writing from *TIME For Kids*.

TIME For Kids and the *TIME For Kids* logo are registered trademarks of TIME Inc. Used under license.

Teacher Created Materials

5301 Oceanus Drive
Huntington Beach, CA 92649-1030
http://www.tcmpub.com

ISBN 978-1-4333-3615-7

© 2012 by Teacher Created Materials, Inc.
Made in China
Nordica.062017.CA21700642

2

Table of Contents

Volcano

Long ago, people thought that powerful gods lived inside **volcanoes**.

The word *volcano* comes from Vulcan, the Roman god of fire.

When the gods were angry, people believed they would spit fire, ash, and **lava** onto the land.

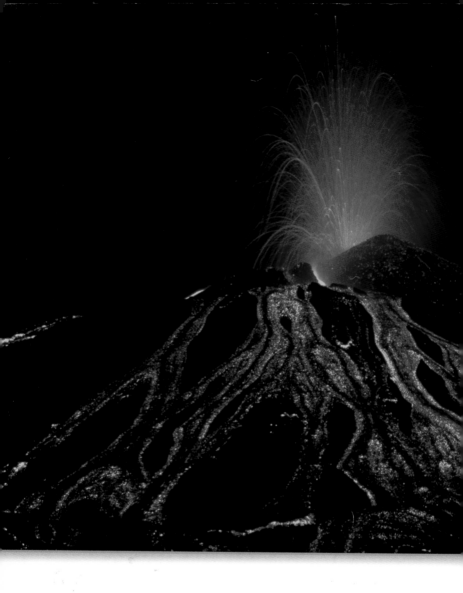

Today, we know that
volcanoes are a part of nature.

Scientists work hard to learn more about volcanoes and why they happen.

Why Volcanoes Happen

A volcano starts as a big, deep hole or crack in Earth's surface. When **pressure** builds, ash, rock, gas, and **magma** escape through the hole. In time, the escaped material can form a mountain.

Magma (MAG-muh) is hot, melted rock.

plates moving

Plate edges are the best places for magma to escape. But if plates are thin enough, magma can push through other holes and cracks in Earth's crust.

rock transformed by heat

Why does this happen?

Earth is made of layers. The outside layer is the **crust**. The crust is made of big pieces of land called **plates**. The plates move slowly against one another.

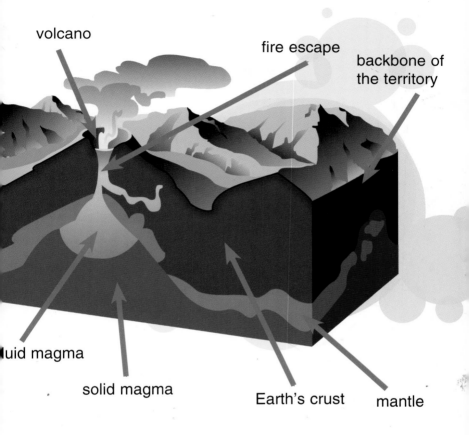

volcano

fire escape

backbone of
the territory

fluid magma

solid magma

Earth's crust

mantle

Under the crust is the
mantle. It is a thick, hot layer
of rock. Deep inside Earth, it is
so hot that the rock melts into
magma.

Pressure and heat in the mantle push the magma into a **magma chamber**. Magma is lighter than the crust, so it tries to push above it.

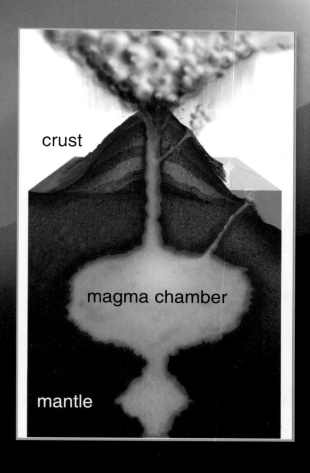

crust

magma chamber

mantle

Finally, pressure from gases pushes the magma through the crust. This is called an **eruption**.

Eruption!

If a volcano might erupt, it is called *active*. If we think it will not erupt now or in the future, it is called ***dormant*** (DAWR-muhnt). Dormant is another word for *asleep*.

An eruption happens when magma, ash, rock, and gases are released from a volcano. Sometimes an eruption comes in a blast. Sometimes it comes in a slow ooze.

Think what happens when you shake a can of soda. When you open it, the soda might blast out or just overflow down the sides. It depends on how much pressure has built up.

The more pressure, the bigger the blast!

Once outside the volcano, magma is called lava. Lava can be fast and runny or slow and thick. Either way, the lava is hot, hot, hot! It can be as hot as 2,012°F.

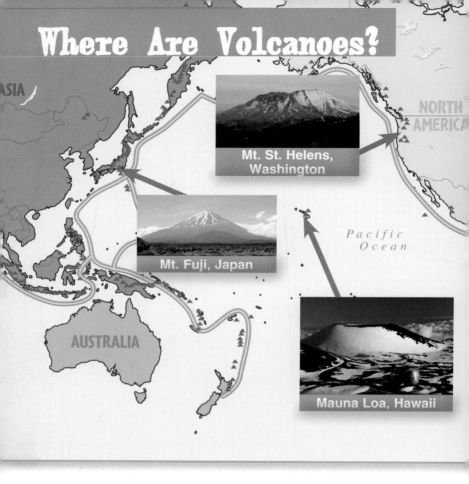

Where Are Volcanoes?

Mt. St. Helens, Washington

Mt. Fuji, Japan

Mauna Loa, Hawaii

Pacific Ocean

ASIA

NORTH AMERICA

AUSTRALIA

There are hundreds of volcanoes all over the world. More than half of them are along the shores of the Pacific Ocean. They are called the Ring of Fire.

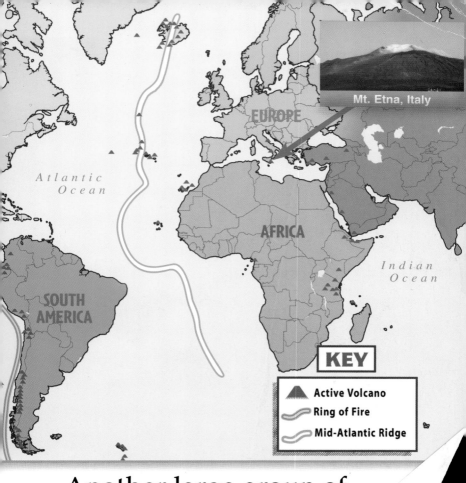

Mt. Etna, Italy

KEY

▲ Active Volcano

Ring of Fire

Mid-Atlantic Ridge

Another large group of volcanoes is found under the Atlantic Ocean. It is called Mid-Atlantic Ridge. It is largest mountain range world!

Earth is not the only place
ere volcanoes are found.
y are on other planets, too.

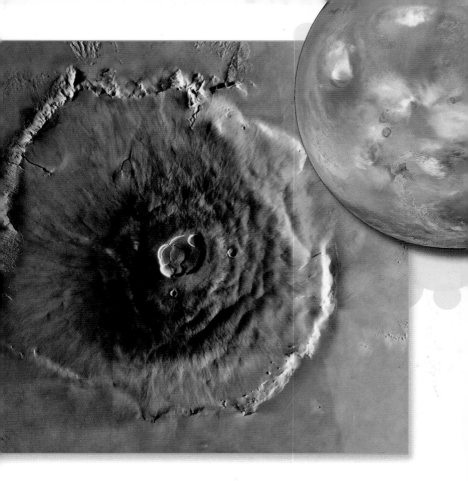

In fact, the largest volcano we know is Olympus Mons on Mars. It is 16 miles tall and as wide as all of Arizona.

Now that's a big volcano!

Glossary

crust—the top layer of Earth

dormant—asleep, not active

eruption—the release of magma, ash, rock, and gases from a volcano

lava—magma that is outside a volcano

magma—hot, melted rock

magma chamber—a pocket within a volcano where magma collects before erupting

mantle—a thick layer of Earth below the crust that is made of gas and magma

plates—large sections of Earth's crust that move, sliding together and apart

pressure—force that builds and pushes against something

volcanoes—areas of land where magma from inside Earth is pushed to the surface and out in an eruption